—PEOPLE TO KNOW—

WILMA
MANKILLER

Leader of the
Cherokee Nation

Della A. Yannuzzi

Enslow Publishers, Inc.

40 Industrial Road   PO Box 38
Box 398   Aldershot
Berkeley Heights, NJ 07922   Hants GU12 6BP
USA   UK
http://www.enslow.com

To my husband, Michael, for his
continued love and support.

Acknowledgments

The author wishes to thank the Oklahoma Historical Society for its cooperation, especially to William D. Welge, Director of the Archives and Manuscripts Division, and Chester Cowen, photo-archivist. Also, thanks to Sandy Reynolds of the Cherokee Nation of Oklahoma; to Kim Malloy; and to Michael J. Yannuzzi for his help as photograph research assistant.

Library of Congress Cataloging-in-Publication Data

Yannuzzi, Della A.
    Wilma Mankiller: leader of the Cherokee Nation / Della A. Yannuzzi
        p. cm. — (People to know)
    Includes bibliographical references (p.) and index.
    ISBN 0-89490-498-1
    1. Mankiller, Wilma Pearl, 1945—Juvenile literature. 2. Cherokee
Indians—Biography—Juvenile literature. 3. Cherokee Indians—
Kings and rulers—Juvenile literature. 4. Cherokee Indians—Politics
and government—Juvenile literature. [1. Mankiller, Wilma Pearl, 1945– .
2. Cherokee Indians—Biography. 3. Indians of North America—Biography.
4. Women—Biography.] I. Title. II. Series.
E99.C5M339 1994
973'.04975'092—dc20
    [B]   93-44866
                                                  CIP
                                                  AC
Printed in the United States of America

10 9 8 7 6 5 4 3 2

Illustration Credits: AP/Wide World Photos, pp. 33, 53, 91; Archives and Manuscripts Division of the Oklahoma Historical Society, pp. 17, 18, 42, 57, 65; Courtesy of the Cherokee Nation, pp. 4, 59, 67, 69, 70, 74, 77, 81, 88; U.S. Department of the Interior, Indian Arts and Crafts Board, Southern Plains Indian Museum and Crafts Center, p. 21.

Cover Illustration: Photo by Gwendolen Cates

Contents

Wilma Mankiller.

1

Doing for Our People

When Wilma Pearl Mankiller, principal chief of the Cherokee Nation, talks, people listen. The more than three hundred Cherokee families living in Bell, Oklahoma, a small town in the eastern corner of the state, are glad they did. They believe Wilma Mankiller's vision for Native Americans saved their town. In a 1991 magazine story, Mankiller shared her optimism and vision for the Cherokee Nation. Without hesitation she affirmed that, "Native Americans can help themselves if given half a reasonable chance."[1]

When Mankiller visited Bell, she was not surprised to find poverty, hopelessness, few educational facilities, inadequate housing, very little indoor plumbing, and lots of anger and frustration. She knew the living conditions of the Cherokees were far from ideal, but instead of feeling despair, Mankiller's determination to offer this community a chance to help themselves grew stronger. The first thing she did was try to organize a town meeting. She was warned by neighboring towns who knew the people of Bell that the residents would never agree to anything she had to offer. The people of Bell had learned to become distrustful due to repeated broken promises made to them. But Mankiller persisted. It took two attempts before anyone would attend her meeting.

Mankiller asked the few people who did show up one very important question. "What change would you like to see first in your town?"

They all answered without hesitation, "We want a water supply to our homes, and indoor plumbing."[2]

Mankiller thought it was a realistic request. For most of us, being able to turn on a faucet and fill a glass with water or take a bath indoors are things we take for granted. But for the people of Bell, Oklahoma, it was something they desperately wanted and needed. The reality was that they did not have indoor toilet facilities or running tap water. Many times, the children had to go to school unwashed because it was too cold to bathe in the streams.

Mankiller, in her straightforward, soft-spoken manner told them she would get the supplies, engineers, and anything else they needed for the water supply and plumbing, but only if they helped raise the funds and build the water system.

There were many doubtful faces that day, and lots of questions. Mankiller could understand their distrust. Experience had taught them that promises were only meant to be broken. How could they believe anyone, let alone another powerless Native American making more unfulfilled promises?

Mankiller's persistence finally convinced Bell's residents that they could trust her and themselves to bring about change. From that meeting, the "Bell Water and Housing Project" was born. It was not long before enthusiasm spread to the remaining skeptical townspeople who began attending the meetings and participating in Bell's new project.

True to her word, Mankiller kept her promises. She wrote grant proposals to get federal funds. She also asked for donations and equipment from private sources to help Bell residents get started on their renewal project. Soon she was drawing the attention of foundation executives who were intrigued by Bell's proposed water system.

The townspeople also kept their promise to help build the sixteen-mile water supply system that would eventually improve their living conditions. Everyone was asked to help. Men, women, and children all had jobs to do which ranged from fund-raising to carrying sand, to installing the pipeline.

Word soon spread about the "big project" going on in the town of Bell. People from surrounding areas came to see what the fuss was all about. Bell even attracted a local television crew that came to film their work. When it ran on the evening news, it attracted even more attention.

It took over a year to finish Bell's water pipeline. The rewards of Bell's success were far-reaching. Not only did the town have running tap water and indoor toilet facilities, but they had also acquired a new sense of pride and self-worth. The local CBS television crew returned to film Bell's success. The story appeared on the CBS news program *Sunday Morning*. The residents of Bell were beginning to feel good about themselves because they were finally being noticed as a community trying to help themselves.

Wilma Mankiller had shown them that wonderful things could be accomplished with lots of determination and hard work. They took her philosophy to heart that people can help themselves if given half a chance. Wasting no time, the people of Bell moved on to their next project. They began work on improving the town's housing. Mankiller, once again, produced the federal funds, but the townspeople had to do the rebuilding.

Bell's achievements were only the beginning for this small community. Since then, they have established an annual fund-raising campaign, an education program to preserve the Cherokee language and culture, a speaker's bureau that presents programs to other towns, and a senior citizens education project. Soon other Cherokee communities began to follow Bell's example. Bell's message rang loud and clear throughout the Cherokee Nation. If the townspeople of Bell could improve their lives, so could others.

Mankiller's belief that people have power over how they face difficult situations is a guiding force in her drive and dedication to help the Cherokees. It was this faith in her people that guided her early years with the Cherokee Nation.

Mankiller can identify with the feeling of being powerless. Her compassion for Native Americans comes from an understanding of past and present Cherokee history and her own personal journey which began at the age of eleven. Her life suddenly changed in October of 1957 when Mankiller and her family left their farm in Tahlequah, Oklahoma. The Bureau of Indian Affairs told them they would have a better life if they relocated to a large city. The goal of the Relocation Program was to have Native Americans mainstreamed into American cities, but for Wilma Mankiller and her family, coping with city living proved to be instant culture shock. They had never seen neon lights, watched television, or ridden in elevators.

Nevertheless, the Mankiller family worked hard to create a better life for themselves. The stories Charley Mankiller told his children about the proud history of the Cherokee people helped them get through some rough times. Mankiller's father kept reminding them that if their ancestors could rebuild their lives when they were forced from their Georgia homeland in 1838, then they would do the same.

Mankiller remembered those family stories. By the time she had reached her twenties, she was following an inner voice which kept whispering in her ear, "We must do for our people."[3]

2

Where It All Began—
In Tahlequah, Oklahoma

Wilma Pearl Mankiller was born on November 18, 1945, at W. W. Hastings Indian Hospital, in Tahlequah (TAL-uh-kwaw), Oklahoma. She was the sixth child in a family of eleven children born to Charley and Irene Mankiller.

Tahlequah has been the capital of the Cherokee Nation for nearly 150 years. The state of Oklahoma takes its name from two Choctaw words: *Okla* for "people" and *homma* for "red." It lies in the south-central part of the United States and is bordered by Kansas, Texas, Arkansas, Missouri, New Mexico, and Colorado. Over sixty Native American tribes live in Oklahoma, more than in almost any other state.[1]

Oklahoma is a land of deep valleys and rivers, grassy plains and prairies, low hills and mountains. It is a state the Cherokees know well, a place they came to when it was called Indian Territory. Wilma and her siblings spent their younger years living in the community of Rocky Mountain in Adair County on ancestral land called Mankiller Flats.

Wilma's father, Charley Mankiller, was a full-blood Cherokee whose family name had been adopted many years ago by an ancestor. He lived on the 160 acres of land allotted to his father in 1907 by the Federal Government, when Oklahoma officially became the forty-sixth state.

Wilma's father traced his heritage back to tribal members who once lived in the Appalachian Mountain regions of Georgia. His family and other Cherokee people had lived there for almost one thousand years, until the U.S. government forced them to "Indian territory," a dry, hot, unfamiliar land.

Wilma and her four sisters and six brothers grew up listening to family stories about the forced removal in the 1830s ordered by President Andrew Jackson, who was not fond of Native Americans. He believed the rich Georgia farmlands and the discovery of gold there by a young Native American boy made the area too valuable for the Native Americans. President Jackson felt the Native Americans should surrender their lands to white settlers and miners. Georgians were also worried because the Cherokee constitution stated that they were an independent people.

The President and state of Georgia were in agreement. Together, they tried to have the Cherokees removed from their lands. In 1828, Georgia ruled that the Cherokee Nation was under Georgia state law, not federal law. The Georgians harassed and arrested, burned, beat, and pillaged the Cherokees for small offenses. Chief John Ross and the Cherokee people pleaded with leaders in Washington, D.C., to help them, but their cries for help fell on deaf ears. Then in 1830, the Indian Removal Act was passed. Many southern tribes were moved to Indian Territory, but the Cherokees resisted through peaceful channels. They continued to appeal to President Jackson and other leaders in Washington, D.C., but to no avail.

Finally, in 1831, the Cherokee Nation asked the U.S. Supreme Court to intervene. The highest Court in the land agreed to hear the case of the *Cherokee Nation* v. *State of Georgia*. Although the Court sympathized with the Cherokee Nation, they did not declare them a sovereign nation, but rather a "domestic dependent nation." The mood of the country reflected such strong anti-Indian feelings that even the Supreme Court could not enforce laws that would protect them. The Cherokee Nation was disappointed, but they were not ready to give up their fight to remain on tribal lands.

Then, an event happened that would change the Supreme Court's previous ruling. An interesting case came before the Court that caused them to reverse their earlier decision made against the Cherokee Nation. When the Reverend Samuel Austin Worcester refused to pledge allegiance to Georgia, he was arrested and sentenced to four years in prison. Worcester appealed to the Supreme Court claiming his rights were denied through the Georgia state laws. In 1832, the Supreme Court found that the law under which Worcester was imprisoned and all the state laws passed as a result of *Cherokee Nation* v. *State of Georgia* were unconstitutional. The Court ruled that the treaties between the United States and Indian Nations were valid, and therefore, the federal government laws superseded state laws within the perimeters of the Cherokee Nation.

President Jackson and the courts of Georgia did not honor the Supreme Court's decision. They persisted in their unfair treatment of the Cherokee people. Even the highest Court in the United States could not protect the Native American.

The Cherokees did everything they could to stay on their ancestral lands, but President Jackson and the state of Georgia were determined to remove them. The majority of the Cherokee Nation refused to leave. They continued to hope for an agreeable treaty. On the other hand, a small group of Cherokees led by Major Ridge, his son, and his nephew wanted to negotiate with Georgia for the Cherokee lands. In October of 1835, a treaty was rejected by the Cherokee Nation, but in December of 1835, Ridge's party signed the Treaty of

New Echota which gave the Cherokee lands to the United States for five million dollars. The treaty also stated that the Cherokees would be moved to Indian Territory within two years. Chief Ross protested the treaty, claiming that it was illegal because it had not been signed by any elected tribal chief or leader. Congress, however, honored the New Echota Treaty.

Finally, in May of 1838, four thousand soldiers and three thousand volunteers rounded up some sixteen thousand Cherokees. They were forced from their homes in Georgia, Tennessee, Alabama, and the Carolinas. The soldiers brought the Cherokees to detention camps to await removal to Indian Territory. The Ani-Yun-wiya, the "Principal People," as the Cherokees originally called themselves, were to be moved by the U.S. military to their new home in the west.

About one thousand Cherokees escaped from the soldiers, disappearing into the Great Smoky Mountains of western North Carolina. They somehow survived, and eventually developed their own government separate from the western Oklahoma tribe.

Unfortunately, the rest of the Cherokees had to leave their homeland. The removal was made in two stages. One group of several thousand moved during the hot summer along a water route, arriving at their destination in winter with no food and little warm clothing. Another larger group waited behind for cooler weather. In the fall they began their twelve-hundred-mile journey, marching westward through a bitterly cold winter. This latter exodus turned into a tragedy when four thousand men, women, and children died on the trail from the cold and illnesses such as pneumonia, smallpox, and cholera. History has chronicled this event as the "Trail of Tears," but the Cherokee called it "The Trail Where We Cried." It is one of the greatest tragedies in American history.

Wilma Mankiller remembers how family members recounted stories of their ancestors being suddenly rounded up without warning and leaving practically everything behind, except for what little they could carry in their arms. Soldiers woke children from naps and separated them from their parents. People were not even allowed to finish their meals. They were ordered to stop whatever they were doing when the soldiers arrived. It is difficult to believe such an event had taken place, but the reality of it was brought home when one of Wilma's aunts showed her a cooking utensil that had been handed down from one of her ancestors who had made that difficult journey.[2]

After the "Trail of Tears," the Cherokee people put their energies into rebuilding their Nation. They established a government, court system, newspaper, and educational system. As long as they had land and the power to self-govern, they were able to remain an independent people.

Then, in 1861, the Civil War broke out and once again brought change to the Cherokee Nation. Divided

This painting depicts the removal of the Cherokees to "Indian Territory" in 1838. This event became known as the "Trail of Tears" because of the many hardships the Cherokees endured along the way.

The Cherokee Female Seminary, in Tahlequah, pictured here in 1889. In addition to a seminary, the Cherokee had their own alphabet and a newspaper written in English and Cherokee.

sympathies within the Nation and the desire for more land by white settlers prompted the government to take Indian Territory. This was only the beginning of a continued downward spiral for all Native Americans.

Unfortunately, the Cherokee Nation and other Native American tribes lost even more rights when the Indian Appropriation Act of 1871 was introduced. This act withdrew recognition of all Native American tribes as independent sovereign nations. This act was then followed by the General Allotment Act of 1877, which gave large areas of Native American lands to homesteaders. It was not until 1907 that the government returned the lands to the Cherokees in the form of small allotments. Then in 1934, the Indian Reorganization Act replaced traditional forms of tribal government with rules and laws controlled by a government agency called the Bureau of Indian Affairs. From then on, the Cherokees, as well as other Native American tribes, were largely dependent on government money and assistance for health care, education, housing, and other social programs.

The Cherokees, of course, were not happy with this situation and tried through the United States courts to regain their independence. In 1946, they were finally recognized by the United States as a nation, and in 1971, they were given the right to self-determination, the freedom to choose their own future political status.

Wilma and her brothers and sisters listened intently

to the stories of hardships the Cherokees were forced to endure. It seemed that her people were constantly challenged to rebuild their lives. This never proved more true than in her own family when the Mankillers were forced to make a decision that would disrupt their lives.

Charley Mankiller and his wife, Irene, who was white and of Dutch/Irish heritage, intended to live the rest of their lives on Mankiller land. They did not have much, but they managed to earn a living by selling strawberries, peanuts, and eggs. Sometimes they traded with neighbors for food they did not grow. Wilma remembers it was a constant struggle making sure the large family had enough to eat.

Basic necessities such as electricity, running water, and indoor plumbing were not a part of the Mankiller's world, but they did have an old 1949 Ford which they all tried to squeeze into for a Sunday drive.

Each morning, Wilma would rise early to do her chores. Sometimes she would gather water at a nearby stream. Other times she would help weed the strawberry patch and pick the strawberries at harvest time. When she finished her chores, she would walk the three miles to school. During her free time, she would roam the woods or listen to her father talk about the Cherokees. What the Mankillers lacked in material possessions was replaced by their close-knit family and their love of living on a land that offered wide-open spaces under a blue prairie sky.

Life in Oklahoma was challenging, but the Cherokees thought it worthwhile. Here, a Cherokee basketry artist of Oklahoma City, works on one of her baskets.

In spite of the uniqueness of the land, earning a living from the farm was not easy. It seemed everything depended on how well the strawberries grew and how much they could sell to put food on the table. As long as they were able to sell their crops, the Mankillers could get by.

But in 1957, things changed drastically for Wilma and her family. For two years there had been little rain in Oklahoma and their farm was failing. Wilma, who was eleven, was old enough to realize the situation was serious. One day, her father had no choice but to go into town and ask for government assistance. Unfortunately, there were not many support programs available to Native Americans in the 1950s. Instead of offering to help them stay in their home, the Bureau of Indian Affairs offered assistance only if they would relocate. The Federal Indian Relocation Program told them they could move to New York, Detroit, Chicago, Oakland, or San Francisco.

After a family discussion, the Mankillers chose San Francisco because Irene Mankiller's mother lived in that area. Charley Mankiller, in particular, was concerned that his family preserve their rich Cherokee culture and language. Would Native American traditions get lost in big city life? In his mind he knew he had to move, but his heart told him he would never forget from where he came.

Wilma acknowledged, years later, that her father

always treasured his Cherokee heritage, no matter where he lived. This strong sense of self also influenced his children. The lively conversations around the dinner table and the strong ties to their Native American culture gave Wilma a keen sense of who she was and what it meant to be a Native American. The foundation for Wilma's future involvement with the Cherokee Nation was established during these early years.

It was not easy to leave friends and family, but one day, in 1957, Wilma and her family boarded a train in Stilwell, Oklahoma. Two days later they arrived in San Francisco, California, ready to begin a new life.

3

A Different Kind of Life

When Wilma had lived in Tahlequah, the thought never crossed her mind that her surname was different or odd. Mankiller was a fairly common name among the Cherokee. She had heard of Whitekillers and Sixkillers, and there was even a lake nearby named Tenkiller. Her father had long ago explained the origin of their family name, which could be traced to an eighteenth-century warrior ancestor called "Mankiller of Tellico." Their ancestor had taken a liking to this name and had adopted it as his own.

Wilma soon found out that although her unusual family name was accepted in rural Oklahoma, it was a different story in a big city like San Francisco. The Mankiller's first stay was in an old hotel until a permanent place could be found for them. Then they were moved to a small apartment in a neighborhood called the Potrero Hill District. Wilma's father and eldest brother, Don, were able to get jobs at a rope factory. Together, they financially supported the family.

It did not take long for Wilma to realize that her Native American heritage and name made her stand out from the rest of the children. The knowledge that her family surname did not merit the same respect in a multiethnic society confused her. Early on, Wilma expressed her dislike for city life and school. She remembers vividly the chanting of her schoolmates as they sang out, "How many men did you kill today, Mankiller?" and the sting of hurt when someone imitated a Native American doing a war dance.[1] She was teased about her handmade clothes, her difficulty with the English language, and the fact that she did not even know how to ride a bicycle.

Coping with prejudice was only one of the problems Wilma and her family had to learn to live with when they moved to San Francisco. The cultural shock of switching from a rural life to city living was like leaving Earth and moving to Mars. One day she was walking to a nearby stream for water, and the next day she was trying to deal with street noises, elevators, bright lights, electricity, and water faucets. Where she had once gone to a neighboring farm to barter for food, she was now being sent to the corner grocery store. Wilma recalled once how terrified she and her brother had been when they heard a siren screeching in the night. They had fearfully clung together, waiting for the horrible sound to stop.[2]

After about a year of living in San Francisco, the Mankillers were able to put a down payment on a small house in a residential community called Daly City, located south of San Francisco in San Mateo County. On the whole, life improved for Wilma. There was more living space, even though Wilma still had to share a bed with her sisters. Also, two other children had been born into the family, now totaling eleven children.

Throughout all these changes, one thing remained constant—Wilma had the love and support of a family committed to getting through the tough times. Communication, respect, understanding, and lively debating in the Mankiller household were a way of life. Wilma learned many valuable lessons from these discussions, one of which was the ability to keep her own individuality.

Wilma and her brothers and sisters gradually adapted to their new environment. They learned to ride bicycles, play hopscotch, roller skate, and jump rope. They worked hard to improve their speech and reading skills and to make friends at the San Francisco Indian Center where they met other Native Americans.

Nevertheless, Wilma was having a particularly difficult time in school. Moving to Daly City meant going to a new school and meeting new people. She worked even harder on trying to lose her Oklahoma accent, but her classmates still teased her about her speech and last name. In addition, her brother Don was going to get married, which meant his income contribution to the family was going to end. Wilma worried about having to move again.[3]

The pressures of wanting to belong and being accepted for who she was overwhelmed Wilma. One day, she decided to run away to her maternal grandmother's home, located ninety miles away in a rural community called Riverbank. Grandmother Sitton, of course, called her parents who came to get Wilma, but in a period of twelve months, Wilma had run off to her grandmother's home at least five times. Eventually, Wilma's parents arranged for her to live with her grandmother, Uncle Floyd, Aunt Frauline, and their four children for one year. In the beginning, there were some normal adjustment problems with her cousins because Wilma was defensive about any comments or teasing directed at her. Eventually, as Wilma's confidence grew, her oversensitivity to casual childhood teasing decreased. At the end of that year, Wilma was a changed person. Country living had agreed with her. Grandmother Sitton had taught Wilma the value of an honest day's work. Even after Wilma returned home, she still visited her grandmother every summer and even after she was married. To this day, Wilma credits her grandmother for helping her to become a more confident, proud, and independent Native American.[4]

Finally, when Wilma arrived home, it was not to Daly City, but to a place called Hunter's Point in southeastern San Francisco. Her brother Don had married and was now living in his own place, so the Mankillers had to find a more affordable house. Hunter's Point was home to a U.S. Navy shipyard and dry docks where Wilma's father found work in a dockside warehouse and became a union organizer. It was also a racially mixed, tough neighborhood of low-income families. There were some Native American families living there, as well as whites, Asians, Samoans, and predominately black families. The sheltered rural life of Oklahoma and the year she had spent on her grandmother's farm were things of the past, replaced by the reality that she was living in a world of people who came from many different ethnic backgrounds. But Wilma had matured. She felt better about herself. She came to realize that with all of its inner-city problems, Hunter's Point taught her invaluable lessons about the importance of getting an education and learning how to live in a multicultural world. It also showed her the strength of people struggling to survive in a world where poverty is an everyday way of life.[5]

Years later, when Wilma was older, she realized that her father was holding the family together by keeping the best of traditional Native American life and culture while taking in the good elements a mainstream world had to offer. Wilma and her brothers and sisters were fortunate to have had parents who believed that although living successfully in two worlds was a difficult goal, it could also be a challenging and realistic one.

Although Wilma's ability to deal with her problems had improved, she was now a teenager and still struggling with her self-image. She did not have many friends in school, but she enjoyed her English courses and took part in Junior Achievement activities. Her salvation though, was the refuge she found at the San Francisco Indian Center which was a source of comfort to her entire family.

At the end of a school day, Wilma would hurry over to the Center and watch TV or talk to the other kids about her problems. There was always something going on for both children and adults. Wilma learned about caring for others at the Indian Center. She had firsthand knowledge about lending a helping hand because her father was always helping others.

Finally, in June of 1963, Mankiller graduated from high school. She had no intentions of going to college at this time. Instead, she moved in with her older sister, Frances, and found a job as a clerical worker for a finance company. But, once again, things were soon to change. Not long after graduation, Mankiller met her future husband at a dance. His name was Hector Hugo Olaya de Bardi, and he was from Ecuador.

Olaya was four years older than Mankiller and very handsome. He came from a prosperous family and was studying business at San Francisco State College. Mankiller and Olaya had fun together going to good restaurants and dance clubs and exploring the San Francisco area. It did not matter to them that their backgrounds and cultures were so very different from each other.

Mankiller had known Olaya for less than six months when he proposed marriage to her. Before she knew what was happening, she accepted. After getting permission from her parents, they flew to Reno, Nevada, and on November 13, 1963, Wilma Mankiller became Wilma Olaya. She was almost eighteen years of age. After a honeymoon in Chicago, the couple settled in San Francisco. Mankiller continued working while Olaya worked at night and took college classes during the day. In January of 1964, Mankiller found out she was two months pregnant. Physically, it was not an easy pregnancy. She began to experience kidney infections that would eventually be diagnosed as a serious hereditary disease. In August of that year, her first daughter Felicia was born, and in 1966, she had her second child, Gina.

Growing up in the 1950s and 1960s, Mankiller did not have many role models outside her family. Her own mother had stayed home to raise eleven children, and Mankiller assumed that she would also become a homemaker. She admits she had no personal ambitions other than to follow traditional female roles. Mankiller enjoyed being with her girls and giving them the time and attention they needed, but in the 1960s San Francisco was a place of free speech, activism, and protest. It was a time when the feminist movement was gaining popularity and women were beginning to question their traditional roles in society. They were becoming more sensitive to social and political issues and wanted a greater voice in the world outside of their homes. Mankiller and many other women were struggling with the idea of how to successfully combine family life with outside work.

During this time, Mankiller and her husband were also beginning to experience problems in their relationship. The differences that existed between them became more noticeable. Olaya wanted a stay-at-home wife with few outside interests, and Mankiller wanted to explore a life outside of the home. Finally, by the late 1960s, Mankiller decided to go to college. She had never enjoyed school, but she knew she had to continue her education in order to move ahead. She enrolled in classes at Skyline Junior College where she took sociology and literature courses. Later, she transferred to San Francisco State College. She also managed to work part-time at different jobs while her family or friends watched her children.

In the midst of all this change, Mankiller was trying

to balance her home life with her outside activities, but in November of 1969, her life would forever be changed. When she heard about some Native American students protesting the way their people were being treated, Mankiller found herself listening to their impassioned cries for help. They called themselves "Indians of All Tribes," and over one hundred of them had taken over the abandoned Federal Prison on Alcatraz Island in San Francisco Bay. They were demanding that Native American lands illegally obtained by the United States be returned to them. They also wanted a new Indian Center established on the island. They refused to leave until something was done to help Native Americans.

Mankiller had found a cause to believe in and decided to show her support. She became a spokesperson and fundraiser on their behalf and began raising money to buy food for the long months they occupied the island. Mankiller claims her involvement with the Native American students opened her eyes to a whole new world. For the first time she realized there were people willing to stand up for the Native American.

For Mankiller, who was then twenty-four years of age, helping the students at Alcatraz Island became a significant, life-changing event. She has best described the Native American students' voices as "validating her own feelings about the injustices Native people have had to endure."[6]

Although the students were unsuccessful in getting

Some of the "Indians of All Tribes" who occupied Alcatraz Island in 1970.

their lands back, they did attract attention to their problems. Mankiller became one of their most loyal and compassionate advocates.

Of course, not everyone approved of this new Mankiller and the direction her life was taking. Still, she could not stand by and ignore the many cries for help coming from the Native American community. Mankiller found herself reevaluating her own life. She was learning about choices and realized that there were many things she wanted to accomplish in life, one of which was to improve the lives of Native American people.

4

Going Home

The early 1970s brought even more change for Mankiller. In 1970, her father began experiencing health problems and was diagnosed with polycystic kidney disease, a genetic condition where cysts form on the kidneys. During her father's illness, Mankiller began experiencing her own health problems, and she too was diagnosed with the kidney disease. Although her illness was not as severe as her father's, the doctors told her the disease would eventually progress and most likely permanently damage her kidneys. She was told to rest, watch her diet, and have regular health checkups. For the time being, there was nothing else she could do.

Dealing with her own medical concerns was difficult enough, but then in February of 1971, Mankiller's father died. He was only fifty-six years old. It was a devastating loss for the Mankiller family, especially for Irene Mankiller, who had defied her family at the age of fifteen when she married Charley Mankiller. The family agreed that Charley Mankiller would be buried in Oklahoma.

Not long after her father's death, the takeover at Alcatraz was over, but Mankiller's involvement with Alcatraz had far-reaching effects. She found she was spending more and more of her time in community work. Her husband resented her being away from home so much, and even insisted she not travel anywhere without him.[1] Mankiller rebelled by withdrawing some money from the bank and buying a car without her husband's permission. Now she was able to travel anywhere, and became even more committed to the Native American community.

One task she took on was becoming the director of the Native American Youth Center in East Oakland. She very quickly displayed her ability for getting things done. She recruited volunteers to help renovate the youth center and immediately initiated many youth programs.

Mankiller was always ready to lend a helping hand. When she heard about the Pit River Indians' struggle with the Pacific Gas and Electric Company over ancestral tribal lands, she volunteered her time by visiting them and researching tribal treaties and laws. On many of these visits, she took her daughters along so they could understand their own Native American heritage.

They visited many other tribes and learned about their customs. Mankiller and her daughters were absorbing invaluable lessons about Native American history and culture.

During these early years of her Native American activism, Mankiller met many people who became her friends and supported her decision to expand her horizons. In order for her to understand these new ideas, she turned to other women for guidance. She joined support groups so she could talk openly about her feelings and concerns. She was encouraged by other women and learned from them that it was possible for people to live their own dreams. She was learning about choices and realized that there were many things she wanted to do in life.[2]

Looking back, Mankiller could not deny that her father's decision to bring his family to California had made certain opportunities available to her that she may never had experienced in Tahlequah. It was clear to her that there would be further choices for her as her life now headed in a new direction.

It was now 1974, and Mankiller knew her marriage of eleven years was over. She and her husband were living separate lifestyles and heading in different directions. Mankiller could not ignore the strong ties she had to her Native American roots, and Olaya could not accept them. He was very much involved in his work as a accomplished businessperson and did not have any interest in changing his busy lifestyle. Finally, Mankiller asked her husband for a divorce. He reluctantly agreed.

Mankiller decided to move with her daughters to Oakland where the cost of living was cheaper. She found a job as a social worker with the Urban Indian Resource Center. During this time, she was planning her return to Oklahoma, but first she needed to save some money. Then an unforeseen complication arose. Mankiller's youngest daughter, Gina, was taken out of the country by her ex-husband and was not returned for nearly a year. When Gina was finally allowed to come by for a visit, she told her mother she wanted to stay with her and Felicia. Mankiller told this to her ex-husband and then left for Oklahoma for a visit. When Mankiller returned to California, she had definitely made up her mind that she would move back to Oklahoma. Her mother had already returned, and one by one her brothers and sisters were returning to their ancestral family lands.

Finally, in the summer of 1977, at the age of thirty-two, Mankiller packed her belongings and, with her daughters, began the journey back to her Cherokee roots. Little did she imagine that she was traveling down a path that would eventually lead her to become the first woman principal chief of the Cherokee Nation and the leader of the second largest Native American tribe in the United States.

Mankiller recalled her decision to move back to

Oklahoma at a March 1993 lecture she gave at the National Museum of Natural History in Washington, D.C. She told her audience that she arrived in Oklahoma driving a rented U-Haul truck with twenty dollars in her pocket and no prospects of a job.[3]

Mankiller and her children lived with her mother in a rented house near the town of Tahlequah, the headquarters of the Cherokee Nation. Within a short time, she was able to build a small log cabin on Mankiller Flats. The surrounding woods and sights and sounds of the outdoors brought back memories of a long ago childhood. Now, all she had to do was find a job.

Although Mankiller has said that she did not set her sights on becoming a political force within the Cherokee Nation, she did have hopes of offering her services to the Cherokee in some way.[4] It was inevitable that she would somehow get involved with working for them.

Armed with some college courses, a working resumé, and a strong record of volunteer work, the Cherokee Nation offered her a job as an economic stimulus coordinator. She was responsible for helping Native Americans become more educated and self-reliant. Part of her job was to write grant proposals for federally subsidized programs, but she soon realized this method would only make the Cherokee more dependent on the U.S. government. One of her goals was to promote economic independence, and the only way she could do this was by encouraging the Cherokee to gain control over their own lives. She wanted them to know that it was possible to generate their own income rather than to depend on handouts from outside sources. Mankiller knew this would not be an easy task to accomplish because of repeated failures in the past, but she was confident it could be done.

"It's a fact that bad things do happen to people," Mankiller says. "We can't always control the unknown, but we can control the way in which we face these difficult situations."[5]

One way in which Mankiller has done this is by setting her sights high for the Cherokee Nation. She firmly believes that people can bring about change, even under terrible conditions. A good example of this strong belief can be seen in the Cherokee town of Bell, once a poor, rural community in Oklahoma. Mankiller encouraged Bell's residents to build the water system that they so desperately needed and wanted. Today Bell is a model community that keeps growing and improving.

Mankiller's hard work and dedication to the Cherokee Nation did not go unnoticed by then Chief Ross Swimmer and the Cherokee council. In 1979, Mankiller was moved into the position of program development specialist and was then responsible for further development of programs that would continue to promote the well-being of Native Americans. She set up job training and educational programs, preschool and adult education classes, and worked with townspeople to improve their communities. A big part of her job was to visit remote rural Cherokee communities and find out how she could best help the people to help themselves. She realized that many Native Americans did not believe things could really change for the better. She was determined to prove to them that they were a competent people who could regain control over their lives. She knew that her new job was going to be difficult. She would have to gain the trust and confidence of the people living in these remote communities, as well as those in Cherokee government.

Mankiller is quick to point out that these programs could not have worked without the cooperation of the Cherokee people, whose teachings tell them that anything positive they do to improve their own lives will benefit those generations coming after them.

Mankiller will be the first to admit that it has been a soul-searching experience to find a balance between the Native American and non-Native American worlds. She has often explained to writers and news reporters that it is a constant balancing act for many Native Americans to reconcile the two worlds. She points out that there are those who have given up on being a Native American and others who embrace their culture so strongly that they refuse to learn English or let their children be exposed to any other cultures.[6]

Although Mankiller had been eleven years old when

Mankiller encourages Native American crafts. Native people have been practicing the art of basket making for many generations.

she moved to San Francisco, she was still able to retain the old traditional Cherokee values and teachings that her father had kept alive for his children. Eventually, as Mankiller grew older, she was able to make her own choices, taking the best of the Native American world and blending it with the best that mainstream America had to offer.

During this time, Mankiller also decided to finish her course work for a college degree in social science. After earning her bachelor of science degree from Flaming Rainbow University in Stilwell, Oklahoma, she decided to begin graduate work in community planning at the University of Arkansas at Fayetteville. Luckily, she was able to take a leave of absence from her job with the understanding that she could return whenever she wanted.

All was going smoothly for Mankiller until one day in the fall of 1979 when she was faced with yet another challenge. She was driving to a class at the University of Arkansas when her car was struck head-on by a car driven by her best friend, Sherry Morris. Mankiller woke up in a hospital bed with severe facial injuries, broken ribs, and crushed legs. It was a miracle she had survived such a terrible car crash.

Mankiller was lucky to have survived the accident, but unfortunately, her friend died. Mankiller did not know this until three weeks later when her friend's husband told her what had happened. Morris had not only left a husband, but a young daughter as well.

Mankiller's recovery was a long and difficult one, lasting for many months. The knowledge that she had lost a close friend in such a tragic accident was only the beginning of a long and painful ordeal.

5

Getting the Job Done

Mankiller has said that her terrible car accident must have been a test of endurance or some kind of special preparation for the work ahead.[1] She admits that the accident made her stronger and more determined to empower herself and the Cherokee Nation to work even harder toward solving their many problems. She also focused on traditional Cherokee wisdom which states that one must always look ahead and try to see the good in the bad.

If Mankiller ever had to prove the wisdom of this philosophy, it was put to the test during her convalescence. Mankiller's prognosis was bleak. At the age of thirty-four, her physicians were not certain that she would ever walk again. For most of 1980, she was in a wheelchair or on crutches. She had to endure seventeen operations, including plastic surgeries to repair the damage to her face and legs. In addition, complications arose when she developed myasthenia gravis, a paralyzing nerve disease which made the tasks of brushing her hair or walking a few steps impossible. At times, she could barely breathe or chew her food. During this period, she fell, re-breaking the bones in her face. More surgery was performed, along with the removal of her thymus to improve the myasthenia gravis. She also had to have high doses of steroid treatment to help fight the nerve disorder.

Soon after the thymus surgery and drug therapy, Mankiller began to feel better. She regained strength in her arms and legs, and her breathing and eating functions gradually improved.

It took Mankiller well over a year to recover, but she had plenty of support from family and friends. In January of 1981, she was ready to go back to work. Wilma's battle to regain her health confirmed her own beliefs that people helping people really works. She had seen it in her own recovery, when family and friends, physical therapists, surgeons, and other professionals had worked with her so she could become a functioning person once again. Mankiller was convinced the best way to emphasize her philosophy was to show the Cherokees that people can solve their own problems if they believe in themselves and work together.

Chief Swimmer agreed that Mankiller could return

to her job. She came back to her work with a renewed enthusiasm. Clearly she was a different person. Although she still had the same positive attitude in her approach to life, the life-threatening car accident had given Mankiller a clearer vision of her goals and what she wanted to accomplish in her service to the Cherokee Nation. She found herself searching out the Cherokee philosophy of life that advocates taking adversity and turning it into a positive experience. She began to draw on an inner, spiritual strength that would enable her to guide the Cherokees out of their social and economical woes.

Mankiller lost no time in establishing her priorities. She continued to write grant proposals but was eager to work with the rural communities. In 1981, she helped to found the Cherokee Nation Community Development Department and was named its first director. Mankiller's goals for the department were clear. She wanted to reach out to Native American communities around the state and find out how she could best serve them. She wanted them to know that they could take an active part in solving their problems if they believed in themselves and worked together.

Mankiller talked about the importance of self-esteem in a biographical article in *Contemporary Heroes and Heroines* which reviewed the incorrect stereotypes that still exist in today's world. She said, "There are far too many movies that depict Indians as savages or just plain lazy, but they are incorrect images. The truth is that

Native Americans are living productive lives in a society that has largely neglected them."[2]

Mankiller strongly believes that stereotyping prevents people from seeing each other as human beings. She describes this blindness as a veil that people look through when they judge different races or cultures.

"If we can only lift this veil and get past the prejudice we can move ahead," she once said in a speaking engagement. "Stereotyping does nothing but hold us back from each other."[3]

Mankiller has studied Native American history and is convinced that Native Americans have to believe they can think for themselves. Only then can they put their positive thoughts into action by becoming involved in rebuilding their homes, improving health care systems, and being trained for decent paying jobs.

"The big job is getting people to say they can," she once said in a news story. "We can do anything if we put our minds to the task."[4]

Mankiller's steady, unswerving service to the Cherokee Nation did not go unnoticed by Chief Swimmer. In 1982, when Swimmer became ill, he asked Mankiller to take his place and attend some meetings in Washington, D.C. Mankiller had to meet with U.S. senators and other officials, and she successfully completed this task.

Then in 1983, when Chief Swimmer's term of office was coming to an end, he asked Mankiller an important question. Would she be his deputy chief when he re-ran for office? This position was equivalent to a vice president's job or second in command.

Although Swimmer was a Republican, and Mankiller was a Democrat, he looked beyond their political differences and realized that they had the same goals for the Cherokee Nation. He saw Mankiller as "having vision and a purpose."[5]

They both agreed that the Cherokee Nation needed self-determination and an independent economic base. Yet, Mankiller could not see herself as a deputy chief, sitting behind a desk. Instead, she said she enjoyed visiting the Native American communities and having daily contact with the people. Chief Swimmer did not pressure her to reconsider. He accepted her refusal.

Then one day, Mankiller saw something that changed her mind. She was driving through the countryside when she saw a Cherokee family living in an abandoned bus. Beside the bus was a clothesline with wash hanging on it. Mankiller's first reaction was that people should not have to live like that. Right then she decided to run for the deputy chief's job. Maybe she could help to bring about change if she was elected into office. That night, Mankiller went to Chief Swimmer's home and told him she would be his running mate.

Once Mankiller had decided to run, she gave it 100 percent effort even though there were others who did not have the same faith in her as Chief Swimmer. It became clear from the beginning that many of the men in the tribe held the traditional view that women did not belong in Cherokee government. People even told Chief Swimmer that his political career would end if he endorsed Mankiller as his running mate.

Mankiller says she was unprepared for the resistance she encountered simply because she was a woman. It was an eye-opener to realize that although she had been accepted as a person doing a good job for the Cherokee Nation, she was not good enough to be an elected official.

It was not an easy campaign, nor was it always a pleasant one. Many people voiced their opinions loudly and openly. They said if Mankiller were voted into office, the Cherokee Nation would be destroyed. Some of her detractors even went so far as slashing her tires and sending her threatening letters. She even remembers being told that the Cherokees would be laughed at by other tribes if she won the election.

In spite of all the opposition, Mankiller was determined to stay in the race. The threats failed to intimidate her. If anything, they made Mankiller stronger and helped her to develop "thick skin." Her previous bouts with illness and near death had prepared her for just about anything. She once told a reporter that if she took everything so personally, she wouldn't be able to do her job.

"I guess you could call me a tenacious individual,"

she admits. "I was raised to believe there were no limitations to what I could do just because I was poor, female and an Indian."[6]

On a lighter side, Mankiller once joked in a *Working Woman* magazine television program that perhaps it was her family name, Mankiller, that frightened men. She feels people get the wrong impression of her as this outwardly aggressive person. However, people who know Mankiller say she is a direct and confident leader who says what is on her mind, but she is also soft-spoken and gentle and has a terrific sense of humor.

Nevertheless, Mankiller viewed her entry into Cherokee government as a step forward and a step backward at the same time. It was ironic for her to see these negative forces at work because she knew that Cherokees were once matrilineal in descent. It had once been acceptable for women to share political power with men and had probably ceased due to the influence of a white male-dominant culture. Mankiller identified strongly with this very important feature of Cherokee history and informed her critics that Native American women in leadership roles were not a new and strange phenomenon.

In the end, despite all the objections, Ross Swimmer and Wilma Mankiller won a close race. In August of 1983, at the age of thirty-eight, Mankiller became the first female deputy chief of the Cherokee Nation. This did not mean she was accepted with open arms by other tribal members. One story Mankiller likes to tell is her early experiences with the tribal council.

One of Mankiller's official duties as a deputy chief was to preside over the monthly council meetings where she would offer suggestions and advice and generally participate in the open discussion. At that time, there were no other women serving on the council. Unfortunately, Mankiller found she was constantly being interrupted whenever she tried to speak. She was told she was not following proper procedures or that she was unaware of the rules governing these meetings. Mankiller tried to be patient, but after continued resistance to her presence at these meetings, she decided something had to be done.

"I had to assert myself," she told an audience during one of her speaking engagements. "Luckily, I controlled the microphones, and each time I was interrupted, I just switched off their mikes. I think those members finally got the message that I was determined to be heard."[7]

In time, things became better. In the two years Mankiller and Chief Swimmer worked together, they were equally committed to improving the Cherokee's economy and social services. Under their leadership, the Cherokee Nation opened a motel and restaurant, a greenhouse, an electronics manufacturing company, and a cattle and poultry ranch.

Then in 1985, Chief Swimmer was offered a position by President Ronald Reagan as assistant

Chief Mankiller, in 1985, when she was appointed to take over Chief Swimmer's remaining two years of office. The Cherokee Nation's emblem is behind her.

secretary of the Interior for Indian affairs. He accepted the offer and left for Washington, D.C. In December of that year, Mankiller was then sworn in as principal chief of the Cherokee Nation, taking over Chief Swimmer's remaining two years of service.

Mankiller suddenly found herself in the number one position. She was more determined than ever to continue working for the Cherokee Nation in the same direct and honest way she had been doing for nearly ten years.

6

Chief Wilma P. Mankiller

In 1986, many exciting things were happening in Mankiller's life, but one of her happiest times was when she married for the second time. Mankiller met Charlie Soap, a full-blooded Cherokee, when he came to work for the Community Development Department at the time she was its director. Charlie had heard of her reputation as a person who liked to get things done. He too was committed to improving the lives of Native Americans. Still, Charlie admits he was a little intimidated by Mankiller's position, but he soon found out she was a fair and hardworking person.[1]

Charlie had been married twice before and had three sons from his first marriage (an infant died in heart surgery) and a six-year-old son named Winterhawk from his second marriage. Charlie and Mankiller found that they had much in common. They were both easy going and shared a genuine concern for the Cherokee people. Mankiller also found out Charlie came from a family of eleven siblings and that his family was well-rooted in Cherokee traditions. He was also fluent in the Cherokee language which helped him to communicate well with the Cherokee. Mankiller was eager to learn more of the language, and Charlie offered to help.[2]

When Mankiller decided to run for chief in 1987, Charlie was by her side through the good and bad times. The year 1987 would prove to be an important one for her. That year, she ran for office on her own, without a popular candidate on her side. Mankiller knew if she was voted into office, it would be based solely on her own qualifications. She felt she had been accepted in the 1983 election because of the popularity of her running mate, incumbent Ross Swimmer. She was determined to change this in the 1987 election through a campaign that focused on her past and present work for the Cherokee Nation. Could she be elected on her own merit? Had Mankiller proved her critics wrong? Did people trust her enough to elect her as the first woman principal chief of the Cherokee Nation?

Mankiller believed the answer to these questions was yes. With that in mind, she became a powerhouse of energy as she threw herself into the 1987 campaign.

From the beginning, it was clear that she was not the favored candidate, even though she had taken over Chief

Chiefs of the Cherokee Nation and Sequoya from 1828–1909. The Cherokee chiefs were chosen by the U.S. government until the early 1970s.

Swimmer's remaining term of office. Her critics still did not feel a woman belonged in Cherokee government, let alone the high office of principal chief. Mankiller needed advice. Did she have a chance at winning? Some people told her she could not possibly win because she was a woman. Others told her she had insufficient funds to run a campaign. But there were many people who supported her, and they told her to "go for it." Eventually, Mankiller made up her own mind. She believed women could hold leadership positions in Cherokee government or any other office for that matter. She decided that gender was not a factor and concentrated on the social issues rather than on the criticism.

With this thought in mind, Mankiller campaigned tirelessly, putting tremendous effort into a campaign which is similar to that of running for the office of President of the United States. She had posters made up and ran television and radio ads. She visited the fourteen counties of the Cherokee Nation. She campaigned door to door. Sometimes she sent out personal invitations or advertised in newspapers for one of her upcoming political rallies. Her husband, family, and supporters helped out in any way they could. Gloria Steinem, one of Mankiller's close friends who was the founder of *Ms.* magazine and a feminist leader, arranged a fund-raiser in New York City so Mankiller would be able to continue her campaign. Charlie Soap contributed by helping to

Mankiller campaigned tirelessly for re-election in 1987.

quiet the fears of many traditional male Cherokees who felt uncomfortable with the thought of a female chief.

Unfortunately, the long hours and hard work took their toll. Mankiller came down with a severe kidney infection and had to stop campaigning while she recuperated in the hospital for two weeks. Doctors told her the polycystic kidney disease was getting worse. Her recurring health problems were now fuel for her opponent, Perry Wheeler. But Mankiller maintained her focus on the issues of health care, self-independence, and unemployment.

In spite of all the difficulties, Mankiller won the election with just 56 percent of the vote. She believes her victory was possible because the Cherokee people finally realized gender didn't matter in determining who was best qualified for the job. In the end, they were more concerned with real issues like health care and reducing unemployment.

Mankiller's philosophy that she could achieve anything she set her mind to was immediately put to the test when she became the elected Cherokee leader. Now, all eyes were focused on Chief Mankiller. The people who voted her into office wanted to see what she could really do.

In July of 1987, at the age of forty-two, Mankiller was sworn into office as the first elected female principal chief of the Cherokee Nation. Although political office was not new to her because of her previous appointment as deputy chief and acting chief, she was very much aware of the significance of being elected to this prestigious position. The responsibilities that came along with the job were enormous. Mankiller and her staff were kept busy developing social programs, health centers, and the tribe's business ventures. By 1990, the tribe's total revenues had increased to over fifty-three million dollars.

Mankiller's priorities were then, as they are today, to encourage financial independence and self-government of a nation that has been dependent on the U.S. government for far too long. During her first term, Mankiller lowered the Cherokee unemployment rate and increased the earnings of the Cherokee Nation businesses by millions of dollars.

Mankiller likes to point out the importance of self-determination for all Native American tribes. She compares the past and present situations of the Cherokee Nation. Although in the 1800s the U.S. government forced the Cherokees out of the Appalachian mountain states, they were still able to recover and prosper from that exodus because the Cherokees had remained a self-governing nation. Yet, they experienced a rapid decline socially and economically when in 1907, the federal government once again took control of the tribe. Today, the Cherokee people are, once again, a sovereign nation.

Mankiller is dedicated to the belief that the

Cherokee people can achieve the same type of prestige and self-government they once enjoyed. History includes numerous Cherokee achievements before their independence was taken away. There were several public schools, including a female Cherokee school, a tribal newspaper, and the Cherokee alphabet, created by Sequoya, the only person in history to create a written language by himself.

Mankiller strongly believes in the connection between the past and present, the old and new. She is working hard to preserve Cherokee culture, history, and beliefs, while at the same time showing that Native Americans can live productive lives in mainstream America.

7

A Hard Day's Work

Wilma Mankiller is the first to admit she puts in a hard day's work at the office. Her fourteen-hour workdays, which often begin at 6:00 A.M. and end between 8:00 and 9:00 P.M., are filled with a variety of duties and responsibilities. They can take her from tackling paperwork in her office at Cherokee Headquarters to getting onto an airplane and flying to a meeting with an important official such as the governor of Oklahoma. For example, one such meeting was with the Oklahoma governor's staff about a plan to tax Native American-owned stores. Mankiller objected to the taxes and pointed out the many contributions the Cherokees have made to Oklahoma in other ways. She hoped that her input would be taken into consideration when a final decision was made.

What is a typical work day for Mankiller? Before daybreak, she can often be found in her home office answering letters or giving her attention to a number of other tasks that are a part of administering the day-to-day routine of the Cherokee Nation.

By 7:00 or 8:00 A.M., Mankiller is usually at her office at tribal headquarters in nearby Tahlequah. The workday can begin with phone calls, paperwork, requests, and meetings involved with the flourishing social programs and businesses spread out among the tribe's fourteen counties and seven thousand square miles of land. Wilma is responsible for nearly 140,000 officially enrolled Cherokees, more than 1,000 employees (91 percent of which are Native Americans), and a 66 million dollar annual budget. She compares her job to that of a president of a small country or the chief executive officer of a major corporation.

After a morning of meetings and other urgent matters, Mankiller may find herself in the tribal government's airplane en route to Oklahoma City for yet more meetings with state leaders. Or perhaps she will be flown to Washington, D.C., where she often lobbies on important Indian issues. Another day may find her working on one of the many problems facing the Cherokee Nation, such as finding solutions to lowering the high rate of unemployment or increasing the average annual salary of a Cherokee which is only $4,300 a year.

When she returns home at night, her work as chief is

Chief Mankiller's busy day may include addressing a group. Here she speaks at the National Capitol Building's rededication ceremony in 1991.

not over. Although she has an office staff of qualified assistants, Mankiller answers business phone calls that she has not had time to get to during her regular workday hours. This may seem like a tremendous job for one person to handle, but Mankiller is aware of the importance and responsibility that comes along with being a leader. She must always remember that on a daily basis, thousands of people are looking to her for guidance. It is a full-time, twenty-four-hour-a-day job.

Mankiller considers all of her duties important, but one of her most challenging is the monthly attendance at the tribal council meetings where important issues are discussed and decided upon. Her deputy chief, John Ketcher, presides over the fifteen-member council, which now includes six women. Mankiller believes honesty and open communication are the ingredients necessary to work successfully with other people. She views her role in these meetings as one of partnership, where the dialogue is open and problems are best solved when everyone is informed and participating.

One of the most important issues voted upon was during a council meeting held in November of 1990. It was an historic event when the council unanimously passed its own criminal code to enforce criminal and civil laws equally, on both Native American and non-tribal land. The reestablishment of the Cherokee tribal judicial system was a major step for the Cherokee

Chief Mankiller attends community meetings where everyone has a voice. Mankiller believes in honesty and open communication.

Nation in their continuing struggle to become a self-governing people.

This monumental decision was not lost on Mankiller. It had been over ninety years since the Cherokee had their own judicial system. With the passing of this law, they would now have a law enforcement system and district courts.

Mankiller is confident that the Cherokee Nation is traveling down the right path in its plan for social and economic independence. Although she is acutely aware of her critics who say she is either too traditional or too nontraditional, she is quick to point out that Cherokee traditions and values are extremely important in maintaining their culture. But she also realizes that people of all races must be open to other cultures as well.

Mankiller speaks from experience because she has lived in two different cultures. She has known for a long time what is important to her and clearly demonstrates her priorities each day in her service to the Cherokee. She admits she consults with a tribal medicine man for spiritual and naturalistic healing advice. She also participates in Cherokee ceremonial practices such as the stomp dancing ritual which is held twice a month on ceremonial Indian ground. She also tries to attend the Cherokee National Holiday celebration held each Labor Day in Tahlequah.

Mankiller strongly believes that people can celebrate who they are, no matter where they go and what they

Wilma Mankiller delivers the State of the Nation address at the annual Cherokee National Holiday. She tries to attend this celebration each year.

Chief Mankiller talking with Senator Daniel Inouye of Hawaii. Senator Inouye is the chairperson of the Senate Committee on Indian Affairs. Mankiller often lobbies for Cherokee issues in Washington, D.C.

do, if they have a strong value system in terms of what is really important to them. Mankiller's inner strength comes from her own belief that things can never seem too hopeless when there is someone or something of a higher force present in your life. This belief is shaped partly from Cherokee teachings that stress the power of positive thinking and inner spiritual influences.

In 1990, when Mankiller was into her third year of office, she was once again faced with a health crisis. The doctors told her that the kidney disease that had plagued her for so many years had finally destroyed her kidneys. She would need a kidney transplant. Mankiller's good friend Gloria Steinem helped to find a doctor to perform the surgery, but first she would need a kidney donor. Mankiller's oldest brother, Don, donated one of his kidneys.

As was proven in the past, Mankiller made a terrific comeback. Within two months after her surgery, she was back at work. But things did not quiet down too much. Before long, she was faced with another serious decision. Her term of office was coming to an end, and Mankiller had to decide whether she would run for reelection in 1991. After speaking with her doctors and her husband, Charlie, Mankiller decided there was just too much unfinished work left to do, so she decided to run for another four-year term. Although running for political office took time away from her family and placed burdens on her health, Mankiller had the support of family, friends, and the Cherokee Nation. On election day, Mankiller captured almost 83 percent of the popular vote. This victory was a testament of the Cherokees' confidence in their chief.

Today, Mankiller is confident that her election into Cherokee government will not only promote women into leadership positions, but also pave the way for men and women to realize that they can work together toward a common goal.

As chief of the Cherokee Nation, Mankiller is always looking for answers and solutions to the problems facing her people. It appears she is on the right track. As one Cherokee tribal member has said, "The Chief is like family. She listens, and is someone you can talk to."[1]

8

Guiding the Cherokee Nation

Today, Mankiller is recognized as a respected leader within the Native American community. She is also well-known by the general population of the United States and Canada. She has been honored with many awards. In 1986, she was inducted into the Oklahoma Women's Hall of Fame, and in 1987, Mankiller received *Ms.* magazine's Woman of the Year Award. In April of 1991, she was awarded the Oklahoma Heritage Award, and in June of 1993, she was honored by the American Association of University Women by receiving their highest achievement award.

Mankiller has also been awarded honorary doctorate degrees from Dartmouth, Yale, Harvard, and Rhode Island College, in addition to many other leadership honors. In spite of recognition for her service to the

Chief Mankiller receiving the Oklahoma Heritage Award in 1991. Mankiller accepts the award from Sanders Mitchell, while her husband Charlie Soap and stepson Winterhawk stand proudly beside her.

Native American community, Mankiller is still confronted with issues relating to her status as a woman leader. One such example that she likes to retell is a funny incident that involves her unusual last name.

"People often wonder how to address me," she once told an audience of nearly two hundred. "A young man I was speaking with began poking fun at my name. He wasn't sure how to address me. Finally I said to him, 'Why don't you just try calling me Ms. Chief as in mischief.' I think that young man was more confused than ever," she ended, smiling.[1]

Chief Mankiller can no doubt stir up lots of mischief in her role as leader of the Cherokee Nation, but instead prefers to take her work seriously, while appreciating the humor in certain situations.

Often, Mankiller has to mix the serious with the humorous in order to maintain a healthy balance in her personal and professional life. There are days when it is difficult for her to believe that she is leading a life so different from the one she saw for herself as a teenager growing up in the Hunter's Point housing project.

She recalls not having many role models, except her parents and maternal grandmother, although she was impressed with Chief Joseph, a nineteenth-century Native American leader of the Nez-Percé tribe who was a man of strong principle and patience.

Another person who influenced Mankiller was Georgia O'Keefe, the American artist who lived to be ninety-eight years old. Mankiller was inspired by a documentary film she saw about this talented painter. She was impressed by O'Keefe's independence and spirit to follow her dream of becoming an artist in a time when few women were encouraged to pursue the arts. Mankiller saw in O'Keefe the ability to follow her own dream and to live the life that she was beginning to envision for herself.[2]

It is ironic to Mankiller that she has become a role model when there were so few for her when she was growing up. She admits to feeling uncomfortable with this status because she doesn't want people to think she is perfect.

"Everyone makes mistakes," she says. "I'm like anyone else. Leaders are not perfect."[3]

Nevertheless, Mankiller is admired for her innovative ideas and the many successful community projects she has started, which include preschool programs, daycare centers, health clinics, community water projects, and a job corps center. Her ability to put in long workdays while balancing a demanding travel and speaking schedule is inspiring to others who are familiar with Mankiller's past injuries and illnesses. Mankiller does not think she is a "superwoman." She is aware of her health problems, yet continues on with her life and work in spite of any setbacks.

Mankiller is constantly thinking about new ways to help improve the quality of life for the Cherokee people.

Chief Mankiller visiting the Cherokee Nation Daycare Center. It is one of the many successful community projects she has started.

Although she knows there are lots of positive changes going on, she is always aware of the fact that more has to be done. She feels a sense of urgency and sums up her feelings in this way, "The youth, especially, are the future. We have to be careful we don't relax too much and watch our future disappear."[4]

One area in which Mankiller would like to see more advancement is in the involvement of more Native American women in higher government positions. She is trying to change the perception that women cannot do a good job in high level positions. Within her own office, she has tried to create an atmosphere of equality and opportunity for women who meet the qualifications needed for a particular job. Her chief of staff is a woman, and there are many other high level positions in the Cherokee offices that are held by competent women.

Mankiller firmly believes that all women should feel a responsibility toward changing those things that they want to see changed. She knows this is not always easy to do. Cherokee girls, in particular, have difficulty seeing how they can play a significant role in the Cherokee community. Sometimes, all that is needed is a little encouragement to send them off in the right direction.

In 1991, Mankiller was given the opportunity to become involved in a project that would increase the skills and self-esteem of Native American girls. Sponsored by the American Association of University Women and the Cherokee Nation of Oklahoma, the

Native American Indian Women and Girls Mentoring Project was initiated to encourage academic achievement for girls in grades nine through twelve.

Mankiller enthusiastically responded to this innovative idea presented to her by Dr. Susan Frusher, a Professor of educational psychology at Northeastern State University in Tahlequah. She directed Dr. Frusher to women in the Cherokee Nation who were working in education, medicine, art, office management, and other fields. Students were then matched with the women working in their areas of interest. The six-month project was an overwhelming success and has continued, expanding to include boys.

It is this kind of program that Mankiller feels Native American youths need in order to build self-esteem and academic excellence. She says ten years ago it would have been impossible for Cherokee girls to aspire to leadership positions.

Mankiller and her husband, Charlie, are committed to a progressive future for the Cherokees. They are personally donating their own time and energy in order to establish relationships with children who are at a high risk of dropping out of school. When Mankiller and her husband can squeeze some spare time from their busy schedules, they invite young people to baseball games and take them to hear other people talk about their own experiences of dropping out of school. In addition to personal contact, Mankiller would like to start a

Cherokee department for children. She has already initiated the building of a new youth shelter across the road from Cherokee Headquarters and has developed summer youth and higher education programs for adults.

Often people wonder about Mankiller's drive and determination. Where does she get her strength to keep moving ahead? Why is she so successful at getting things done?

Chief Mankiller says she just follows the teachings taken from older, wiser Cherokees. Traditional Cherokee philosophy believes that everyone should have a good mind. When translated, this means that you have to look for the good rather than the bad in people and in situations.

Another Cherokee teaching states that everyone is dependent on each other and must think not only of themselves, but of others as well.

And finally, the Cherokee are taught to look to the future and think about their actions and how it will affect future generations.

Mankiller appears to be following these teachings. They are reflected in her everyday life and leadership qualities. People who know her give their own reasons as to why they think she is doing such a good job.

Don Greenfeather of the tribal employment rights office is convinced Mankiller's low-key, humble manner establishes her as a great stateswoman. "She doesn't brag

Chief Mankiller busy at her desk in Cherokee headquarters.

about her successes, although she has helped to establish the Cherokee Nation as a people regaining control of their lives."[5]

Pat Ragsdale, a U.S. Bureau of Indian Affairs executive thinks, "Mankiller is an excellent leader who has the ability to carefully listen to problems and then find ways to solve them."[6]

While most of Mankiller's time is given to the day-to-day concerns and administration of the Cherokee Nation, she does have another life away from her work. Chief Mankiller has a large family. In addition to her two daughters, Gina and Felicia; three stepsons, including Winterhawk who lives with her; her mother who lives close by; and her siblings, nieces, and nephews, Mankiller is also a grandmother of three boys and one girl. At the end of a long workday, she enjoys returning to the peacefulness of her simple log cabin in the woods of Adair County. It is here that she often takes long walks with her husband, and their pet dogs.

Inside her home, Mankiller is surrounded by handwoven Native American baskets hanging on the walls and many good books. Whenever she can find the time, she likes to write and has had short stories published. One story entitled "Keeping Peace with the Rest of the World" was printed in 1985 in a magazine called *Southern Exposure*. It is a story about young Cherokees who want to get away from Native American traditions. Wilma also likes to cook and has written a cookbook called *The Chief Cooks*.

Another project in which Mankiller is involved is the co-editing of a Reader's Companion book on the history of women in the United States. Her autobiography, which she co-wrote with Michael Wallis, has also been published. It is called *Mankiller, a Chief and Her People*, in which she writes not only about her life and struggles, but also about the history and struggles of the Cherokee people.

Chief Mankiller often wonders about her future and that of the Cherokee people. When the time comes for her to move on to other things, she will carefully make her decisions, but for now, she is concentrating on her job as leader of the Cherokee Nation.

9

Marching Into the Future

In an article published in *Native Peoples* magazine, Mankiller best expressed her feelings for the Cherokee Nation.

> Our languages are strong, our ceremonies remain, our culture and governments are surviving. Our people are looking for solutions within their own communities. We look forward to the next five hundred years as a time of renewal and revitalization for Native people.[1]

One of Mankiller's main goals for the Cherokees has always been sovereignty, which means giving people the right to self-government with very little outside control. As a sovereign nation, federally recognized tribes have their own government and tribal laws. This idea, called self-governance or self-determination, is nothing new to

Native Americans. They did not cease to be an independent people of their own free will.

Mankiller's views on the importance of self-governance are clear and concise when she says, "What we want and need is more control over our lives. Look at where we are today in comparison to the last one hundred years."[2]

The Cherokee Nation's growing list of achievements becomes more impressive with each passing year. Yet, Mankiller refuses to become complacent. Although she is confident the Cherokees are heading down the right path, she believes there are more bridges to be crossed.

One successful crossing was the 1990 agreement with the U.S. government for appropriation of 6.1 million dollars in federal assistance funds, which had been previously controlled by the Bureau of Indian Affairs. This transfer of funds will allow the Cherokee Nation to have direct control over how the money is spent and invested. Chief Mankiller and the tribal council have already earmarked these resources for new construction projects and businesses.

Another major breakthrough for the Cherokees was the reestablishment of a tribal judicial system which gave the Cherokee government authority to enforce their own civil and criminal codes, although tribal laws cannot supersede federal law.

A remaining struggle still facing the Cherokees and other Native Americans is the reclaiming of their lands and having more control over environmental concerns. When Native Americans lost their ability to self-govern, they also lost the laws that protected their lands from pollution. Because their lands were called Indian reservations, they were excluded from environmental laws. This lack of protection left America's 287 Indian Reservations open to all kinds of polluting. While the early, original Clean Air Act, Clean Water Act, and Solid Waste Disposal Act were trying to protect non-Native American lands, Native Americans were suffering at the hands of violators who were dumping their wastes in Native American country.

Mankiller and other Native American leaders have taken an active part in cleaning up the environment. The Cherokees have their own environment office and geologist and work with other tribes to keep water safe and clean. Funding has also helped Mankiller to hire specialists to identify and clean up waste sites. She is currently working on a dispute against the federal government that deals with the polluted Arkansas River which the Cherokee Nation partly owns. Until this is resolved, Cherokees can't drink water from their own wells due to contamination.

The return to self-government is a common goal shared by the Cherokees, as well as by other Native American tribes, but sometimes non-Native Americans have trouble understanding why Native people can't be like everyone else. Why must they have their own government and their own laws? Can't they just be Americans, existing under one government?

Mankiller addressed this issue during one of her speaking engagements. She told the audience that Cherokee government is not so different from the United States government but reminded them that the Cherokees had their own government well before the United States had theirs. She added that a study of the history of failed relations between the U.S. government and Native people needed to be understood in order to fully appreciate why sovereignty is so important to Native Americans.

Mankiller knows that self-determination for non-Native Americans can be a sensitive issue. There are very few full-blood Cherokees anymore because of intermarriage, but this does not mean they are any less proud of their heritage. Many Native Americans live and work in mainstream society but still live by traditional Native American values and remain active in Cherokee cultural customs and events.

As chief of the second largest Native American tribe in the United States, Mankiller is constantly trying to set an example for Native people who want to live in the present yet need to retain their proud Native American past. She best defines being a Cherokee as someone who is willing to be a part of a society, a person who cares about others and who has a positive attitude no matter what the circumstances.

Chief Mankiller signs the 1992 self-governance agreement which states that the Cherokee Nation is a sovereign nation once again.

Mankiller puts into practice her beliefs. She is a leader who cares about others and who maintains a positive attitude. These attributes are visible in her leadership skills and the continuing social and economic growth of the Cherokee Nation. The future is full of promise for the Cherokees. Chief Mankiller and the tribal council are making plans well into the future. Some of the proposed projects that are currently being worked on include the building of a nine million dollar vocational training center and the making of Cherokee language computer programs that will be available in public schools. There are also plans to expand summer youth programs and to begin school programs for older women.

Another priority on Mankiller's list of "must do's" is the continuing need to provide good health care for the large Cherokee population. The Nation has already established five health care centers, and a mobile unit is available to those people who cannot come to the centers. About one-third of Mankiller's time is spent on health care issues.

Another major social problem that is facing the Cherokee Nation is the high alcoholism rate, but Mankiller is encouraging participation in youth sobriety programs. She views these programs as a good example of people taking charge and solving their own problems.

Another area that Mankiller continues to develop is

the Cherokee Business Corporation, which is a group of businesses employing the Cherokees and generating income for the Nation. One of their most successful ventures has been a Cherokee electronics plant which manufactures equipment for the Department of Defense. It grosses over twenty-four million dollars annually. Their greenhouse business is also flourishing with over forty stores in regional shopping malls. The proportion of the Cherokee Nation's income coming from business revenue has increased to 60 percent, where they were once 90 percent dependent on federal assistance.[3]

Mankiller learned early on in her work with the Cherokee Nation that although social reform programs were desperately needed, the need for financial independence was equally as important. Native Americans have found out that private enterprise can be a way out of poverty. Her critics even took notice of her when she was able to increase the tribe's revenues.

The issue of financial independence is so important to Mankiller that when she was invited to speak at President-elect Bill Clinton's Economic Conference in December 1992, she quickly packed her bags and traveled to Little Rock, Arkansas. When it was her turn to speak, Mankiller made a strong appeal for more economic opportunities for Native Americans. She said her biggest concern was the national average

Chief Mankiller at a health care reform meeting with First lady
Hillary Clinton and Senator Inouye in March 1993.

unemployment rate on Indian reservations which stands at over 50 percent, a much higher rate than even the 20 to 30 percent rate during the Great Depression. Mankiller made a plea for businesses to invest their money in Native American-owned small companies.[4]

"Speaking as a person trained in social work, I believe the best hope we can offer to people is a job," she told the National Economic Policy Panel. "We have to look at poor people in a different way. They want to help themselves, and we want to help them, but we also need your assistance in developing the economy of Native American communities."

Although Mankiller envisions Native Americans making great strides as they move into the twenty-first century, she is also a realist and knows that all of the problems facing her tribe will not be solved immediately. But for today, she is trying to focus on the most pressing concerns facing her people, and they are repaying her with their trust and respect.

Mankiller has decided that she will not seek re-election when her term as Principal Chief of the Cherokee Nation ends. She believes it is time for a change, both for herself and the Cherokee people.[5] What will she do when she is no longer the leader of the Cherokees? Will she run for another political office such as a senator's seat or even for governor of her own state? Will she accept teaching offers which she has already received?

There is no doubt in anyone's mind that whatever road Chief Wilma P. Mankiller decides on will be of her own choosing. She is definitely a woman committed to her people, a woman who has placed no limits on herself or the Cherokee Nation.

Chronology

1945—Wilma Pearl Mankiller is born at W. W. Hastings Indian Hospital in Tahlequah, Oklahoma.

1946—The Cherokee people are recognized by the United States as a nation.

1957—The Mankiller family relocates to San Francisco.

1963—Mankiller marries Hector Hugo Olaya de Bardi.

1971—Mankiller's father dies; U.S. government gives the Cherokee Nation the right to self-determination.

1974—Mankiller and her husband divorce.

1977—Mankiller and her daughters move back to Oklahoma; goes to work for the Cherokee Nation.

1978   Mankiller earns her B.S. degree from Flaming Rainbow University in Stilwell, Oklahoma.

1979—Mankiller is in a car crash with her friend Sherry Morris; Morris is killed, and Mankiller is severely injured.

1980—Mankiller develops myasthenia gravis, a paralyzing nerve disease.

1981—Mankiller returns to work at the Cherokee Nation; becomes the first director for the Cherokee Nation Community Development Department.

1983—Chief Ross Swimmer asks Mankiller to be his running mate when he seeks his third term of office. They win the race, and Mankiller becomes deputy chief.

1985—Wilma P. Mankiller becomes the first woman principal chief of the Cherokee Nation, filling remaining term of Ross Swimmer.

1986—Chief Mankiller marries Charlie Soap, a full-blooded Cherokee; also inducted into the Oklahoma Women's Hall of Fame.

1987—Mankiller runs for the office of principal chief and wins the election.

1990—Chief Mankiller signs the self-determination agreement with the U.S. government; also has a kidney transplant.

1991—Mankiller runs for another four-year term as principal chief of the Cherokees.

1992—Chief Mankiller attends President-elect Bill Clinton's National Economic Summit in Little Rock, Arkansas.

1993—Mankiller is honored by the American Association of University Women by receiving their highest achievement award; her auto-biography, *Mankiller, A Chief and Her People* written with Michael Wallis, is published.

1994—Mankiller announces she will not seek re-election when her term ends in 1995.

Chapter Notes

Chapter 1

1. Hank Whittemore, "She Leads a Nation," *Parade Magazine*, (August 18, 1991), pp. 4–5.

2. Gloria Steinem, "A New Kind of Leader," *Ms.*, (November/December 1991), p. 29.

3. Rod Davis, "Trail of Triumph," *American Way*, (January 15, 1988), pp. 58–62.

Chapter 2

1. Rita C. La Doux, *Oklahoma*, (New York: Lerner Publications Co., 1992), p. 42.

2. Hank Whittemore, "Wilma Mankiller," *Parade Magazine*, (August 18, 1991), pp. 4–5.

Chapter 3

1. Ponchitta Pierce, "Still Trying to Fight It," *Parade Magazine*, (January 3, 1993), p. 9.

2. "Chief of the Cherokee," *Southern Living Magazine*, (November 1986), p. 190.

3. Wilma Mankiller and Michael Wallis, *Mankiller, A Chief and Her People*, (New York: St. Martin's Press, 1993), pp. 103–105.

4. Ibid.

5. Ibid.

6. David Van Biema, "Wilma Mankiller–First Female Chief of the Cherokee Nation," *People Weekly*, (December 2, 1985), p. 13.

Chapter 4

1. Wilma Mankiller and Michael Wallis, *Mankiller, A Chief and Her People*, New York: St. Martin's Press, 1993, p. 201.

2. David Van Biema, "Activist Wilma Mankiller Set to Become First Female Chief of Cherokee Nation," *People Weekly*, (December 2, 1985), pp. 99–92.

3. Speech by Wilma Mankiller, Celebrating Women in History Month at the National Museum of Natural History, Washington, D.C. (March 24, 1993).

4. Jeanne M. Devlin, "Hail To The Chief," *Oklahoma Today*, (January–February 1990), pp. 34–37.

5. Mary Crescenzo Simons, "Wilma Mankiller, Cherokee Chief," *Highlights for Children*, (April 1993).

6. Leslie Sowers, "Wilma Mankiller, Chief of the Cherokees," *Texas Magazine*, (January 20, 1991), pp. 12–13.

Chapter 5

1. Hank Whittemore, "She Leads a Nation," *Parade Magazine*, (August 18, 1991), p. 5.

2. *Contemporary Heroes and Heroines*, 2nd ed., Detroit: Gale Research, (May, 1992).

3. Speech by Wilma Mankiller, Celebrating Women in History Month at the National Museum of Natural History, Washington, D.C. (March 24, 1993).

4. Elizabeth Levitan Spaid, "Rebuilding a Nation," *Los Angeles Times*, Sunday Home Edition, (October 4, 1992), p. 6.

5. Leslie Sowers, "Wilma Mankiller, Chief of the Cherokees," *Texas Magazine*, (January 20, 1991), pp. 10–14.

6. Speech by Wilma Mankiller, Washington, D.C. (March 24, 1993).

7. Ibid.

Chapter 6

1. Leslie Sowers, "Wilma Mankiller, Chief of the Cherokees," *Texas Magazine*, (January 20, 1991), p. 13.

2. Wilma Mankiller and Michael Wallis, *Mankiller, A Chief and Her People*, (New York: St. Martin's Press, 1993), pp. 235–237.

Chapter 7

1. Leslie Sowers, "Wilma Mankiller, Chief of the Cherokees," *Texas Magazine*, (January 20, 1991), p. 14.

Chapter 8

1. Speech by Wilma Mankiller, Celebrating Women in History Month at the National Museum of Natural History, Washington, D.C. (March 24, 1993).

2. Joanna Biggar, "Cherokee Chief Fills Many Roles in Life," *Daily Oklahoman*, (May 13, 1993).

3. Speech by Wilma Mankiller, Washington, D.C. (March 24, 1993).

4. Lola Shropshire, "Cherokee Chief Wilma Mankiller," *Twin Territories*, vol. 2 no.1, (1992).

5. Elinor L. Horwitz, ed., American Association of University Women, *OutLook* vol. 87 no. 1, (Spring, 1993) pp. 6–9.

6. Leslie Sowers, "Wilma Mankiller, Chief of the Cherokees," *Texas Magazine*, (January 20, 1991), pp. 10–14.

Chapter 9

1. Rayna Green, *Women in American Indian Society*, (Chelsea House Publications, New York: 1992), p. 99.

2. Leslie Sowers, "Wilma Mankiller, Chief of the Cherokees," *Texas Magazine*, (January 20, 1991), p. 12.

3. Robert H. White, *Tribal Assets*, (Henry Holt & Co., New York: 1990), p. 271.

4. Chief Wilma Mankiller, Speaker at the Clinton–Gore Economic Conference, Little Rock, Ark., (December 14–15, 1992). Text publications by Donald I. Fine, Inc. New York pp. 297–299.

5. "Cherokee Losing Chief Who Revitalized Tribe," *The New York Times*, April 6, 1994, p. A16.

Further Reading

Anderson, William L. *Cherokee Removal, Before and After.* Athens, Ga.: University of Georgia Press, 1991.

Ehle, John. *The Trail of Tears, The Rise and Fall of the Cherokee Nation.* New York: Anchor Books, Doubleday, 1988.

Green, Rayna. *Women in American Indian Society.* New York: Chelsea House, 1992.

Landau, Elaine. *The Cherokees.* New York: Franklin Watts, 1992.

Lepthien, Emilie U. *The Cherokee.* Chicago: Children's Press, 1985.

Mankiller, Wilma and Michael Willis. *Mankiller, A Chief and Her People.* New York: St. Martin's Press, 1993.

Morgan, H. Wayne and Anne Hodges. *Oklahoma—A History.* New York: W. W. Norton & Co., 1977.

President Clinton's New Beginning. Text of the Clinton–Gore Economic Conference. December 14–15, 1992. New York: Donald I. Fine Inc., 1993.

Steinem, Gloria. *A Book of Self-Esteem, Revolution From Within.* Boston: Little, Brown & Co., 1993.

White, Robert H. *The Rebirth of Native America.* New York: Henry Holt & Co., 1990.

Index